SMITHSONIAN
National Air and Space Museum

AMERICA'S HANGAR

I t is my distinct pleasure to welcome you to the Steven F. Udvar-Hazy Center, named for the museum's main benefactor. With the opening of the Center, the Smithsonian Institution's National Air and Space Museum may now display the largest collection of air and space craft from around the globe in a single location at Washington Dulles International Airport—it is America's Hangar.

Unveiled within this colossal structure is the first installment of more than 300 aircraft and spacecraft that will be displayed on three different viewing levels in two separate, immense hangars over the next five years. What you are witnessing is a work in progress—the realization of a dream conceived decades ago to display the majority of our air and space treasures for all to enjoy.

The museum features craft from all eras of flight and from many countries. The Lockheed SR-71 on display is a world speed record holder and is still the fastest aircraft ever built. America's newest military aircraft, the Lockheed-Martin X-35B—the first aircraft in history to accomplish a short takeoff, supersonic run, and vertical landing on one mission—will also rest here. A spectacular collection of foreign and U.S.-built rockets and spacecraft from World War II through the present will be featured throughout the Center and eventually find their permanent place in the James S. McDonnell Space Hangar, home to the space shuttle *Enterprise.* In the meantime, famous air and space craft—like the *Winnie Mae,* Concorde, Boeing B-29 *Enola Gay,* and the Laser 200— can now be viewed as never before.

This new Center and the National Mall building are really one gigantic air and space museum separated only by distance. The visitor experience, however, is completely different in each. The Center's open hangar-like design allows us to display aircraft that could not even fit through the doors of the National Mall building. Looking skyward, the open ten-story structure allows us to display many of our collection in exciting realistic ways. It will be hard to forget the Curtiss P-40, hung as if attacking a convoy, or the inverted-gull-wing Vought Corsair, ready to "catch a wire" on an aircraft carrier. The aircraft that brought American passenger planes into the jet age, the Boeing 367-80, will also rest here. Though different, the combined museum experiences are complementary. The galleries in our original museum on the National Mall explore air and space flight throughout the ages in a more traditional, exhibitions-oriented way. America's Hangar is an awe-inspiring open showroom of amazing and rare air and space artifacts.

Think of this new museum as a centennial anniversary present and tribute to aviation and space exploration. It was one century ago that the Wright brothers flew for the first time. The first flight was only slightly shorter than the wingspan of the B-29 on display, but what a beginning! In this hangar you will find the history of aviation that was born on that windy December 1903 day on the sands of Kitty Hawk. Enjoy your visit!

J. R. Dailey
Director
National Air and Space Museum
Smithsonian Institution

The aluminum-panel-clad theater, elliptical observation tower, and fuselage-shaped entrance are unique architectural features of Hellmuth, Obata + Kassabaum's design of the Udvar-Hazy Center. Courtesy Sisson Studios.

Planning, Design, and Construction of the

In July 1976, 30 years after Congress authorized the establishment of the National Air Museum as part of the Smithsonian Institution, the National Air and Space Museum (NASM) opened the doors of its flagship museum on the Mall in Washington, D.C. Even as the Museum's staff was moving historic aircraft into this space, they realized that they would need a second facility to house the growing National Collection of aviation and space artifacts. The new building was large—three city blocks long—but the largest aircraft being relocated there was a Douglas DC-3, which started its flying career in 1936. How could the Museum tell the history of modern aviation and spaceflight? Where could the Museum display the next generation of commercial airliners? How could the Museum ever bring the space shuttle *Enterprise,* which had just rolled off the assembly line, to downtown Washington?

Steven F. Udvar-Hazy Center

As early as the mid-1960s, proponents of a national air museum had been suggesting that the new Washington Dulles International Airport could meet the needs of the Smithsonian: it was within an hour's commute of the tourists who came to Washington; its runways were suitable for the arrival of large aircraft; and there was acreage available for long-term growth. But the Smithsonian and Congress first supported the construction of an aerospace museum in downtown Washington as part of the Institution's popular complex of museums. In this location, NASM has consistently attracted more visitors than any other museum in the world, routinely hosting more than 9 million visitors annually.

Before the Museum was built, the Smithsonian displayed aviation and space artifacts in a temporary building on the Mall and at the Arts and Industries Building, but the majority of its collection was stored, unseen, in Suitland, Maryland. Many of the aircraft had been at this cleared forested swamp in an area called Silver Hill, waiting for better quarters since the early 1950s. When the new Museum opened in 1976, however, many artifacts were left behind. And as the collections continued to grow, the 21-acre complex could not provide the quality of care museum artifacts deserve. NASM revived the idea of taking part of the collection to Dulles.

Throughout the 1980s, NASM made its case that a second facility at an active airfield was required to guarantee the future of its important collection. Dulles met all the Museum's requirements, including the support of airport and local authorities. In 1984, the Smithsonian submitted its first Congressional request for authorization to

OPPOSITE
The Udvar-Hazy Center is located on 176.5 acres in the southeast quadrant of Dulles International Airport, with easy access to a nearby runway and major highways.

ABOVE
Christine and Steven F. Udvar-Hazy on a tour of the construction site, April 2, 2002.

Hensel Phelps Construction Co. built the huge aviation hangar in less than two years. ADF International, the structural steel subcontractor, partially fabricated the huge trusses at the factory and finished the job on-site.

Crane operators took each finished truss section to its designated location in the 984-foot-long hangar.

ADF bridged the trusses together in groups of four.

Using two cranes, the construction team raised the truss sections in place as a single unit.

Center truss sections were installed one by one.

ADF raised the first truss sections in late January 2002 and bolted together the final center section five months later.

Each of the 21 trusses in the vaulted hangar can accommodate the weight of two World War II fighter aircraft.

The Center's design reflects the airport environment.

build at Dulles. It took nearly a decade for lawmakers to pass legislation and provide funding. During those years, the collection had continued to grow, artifacts stored in substandard conditions had continued to degrade, and construction prices had soared. Encouraged by a guarantee of financial support from the Commonwealth of Virginia, Congress approved $8 million in 1993 to design the "Dulles Extension." Three years later in a second bill, Congress further authorized the Museum to proceed, but with the caveat that no federal money be spent on construction.

The Smithsonian had already begun to formally define its needs for the new facility. Hellmuth, Obata + Kassabaum (HOK), the architectural firm that had designed the Museum on the Mall, was again engaged to assist the Smithsonian. Working with collections experts, curators, and exhibit designers, HOK produced reports that quantified the facility in terms of size, structural and mechanical requirements, site and access needs, and environmental impact. By the time Congress approved design funds, airport officials had identified a 176.5-acre tract of land in Dulles' southeastern quadrant that was ideal for the Museum: less than a mile from a north-south runway, close to major highways, and with room for growth.

HOK and the Museum remained true to their original concept for a building that would meet the special needs of a large collection of aircraft and spacecraft—along with millions of visitors—but still fit the ambience of an airport. The design featured a large vaulted space, reminiscent of a dirigible hangar, for some 200 aircraft. The Museum told the designers that they wanted to hang many aircraft as if they were flying, and they needed to get the most display space for each construction dollar spent. The space shuttle *Enterprise,* along with some 135 other space vehicles, would be housed in the James S. McDonnell space hangar. Visitors would also be able to watch specialists restore aircraft, conduct research in the archives, take classes in an education center, and watch IMAX® movies. The total complex logged in at 760,000 square feet. While the Museum could have used even more space, officials understood the enormous fund-raising task ahead of them and approved a design that met their most immediate needs.

As part of a generous contribution from Virginia, the state funded all the site infrastructure needs of the project. In the spring of 2000, the Virginia Department of Transportation (VDOT) let a contract to clear land for the "Dulles Center." The land upon which the new facility would be built had been farmed since the Colonial period. When

Another team of steelworkers built the frame for the IMAX® theater.

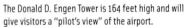

The Donald D. Engen Tower is 164 feet high and will give visitors a "pilot's view" of the airport.

the airport bought the property in the 1950s, it planted the fields in pine trees, which were ready for harvesting when the contractors came onto the site. In the fall of 2000, the Smithsonian officially broke ground and honored the benefactor after whom the project was newly named: Steven F. Udvar-Hazy.

As the Smithsonian awarded the building contract to Hensel Phelps Construction Co. (HPCC) in the spring of 2001, VDOT sent in their second contractor team to complete utility installation, pave roads and the 2,000-car parking lot, and complete a link to Runway 1R-19L. Because the Institution was raising funds for construction while construction was ongoing, the Museum phased the project. HPCC would first build the huge aviation hangar and the architecturally stunning east wing, which would contain the theater, classrooms, food court, and other assets required by the 3 to 4 million visitors expected each year. The initial contract was let for $125,578,000. With an army of subcontractors, HPCC set two teams to work: one on the east wing and one on the hangar. Each worked north to south. Blessed by a dry, mild winter, construction crews flew through their schedule. The mighty hangar trusses, each of which could support the weight of up to two World War II fighters, were erected in less than six months. In April 2002, construction began on the space hangar. By the fall of 2002, the project under contract was more than three-quarters complete. Opening day, in December 2003, is timed to celebrate the anniversary of the Wright Brothers' first flight on December 17, 1903.

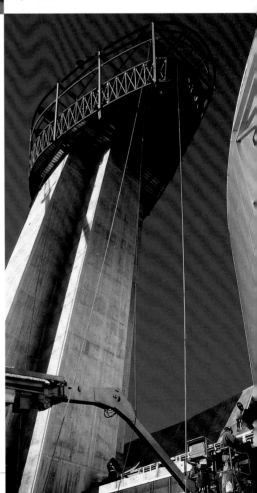

TOP

Presentation case with Naval Aviator Badge, Navy Cross, Distinguished Flying Cross, and Air Medal

Presentation case with all of VADM Engen's Rank insignia and medal ribbons

Piece of deck from USS *Boxer* (first night landing of a jet a/c onto an aircraft carrier)

Logbooks from Navy flying

Autobiography *Wings and Warriors*

Flying helmet Type APH-6B

Flying jacket Type L-2

BOTTOM

War bonnet "Chief Sky Warrior" presented by Kiowa Tribe

NTSB badge and credential

FAA badge and pilot's license signed as FAA Administrator and pilot

Appointment to FAA and pen used by President Reagan to sign appointment

Pilot's logbooks

NBAA Trophy

Doolittle Trophy

ABOVE
The Donald D. Engen Observation Tower under construction.

BELOW
VADM Don Engen, USN (Ret.) next to the model of a vision—the Udvar-Hazy Center.

Donald D. Engen
Observation Tower

DONALD D. ENGEN, the late Director of the National Air and Space Museum (1996–1999), was a tireless advocate of the need for the Udvar-Hazy Center. In 1984, he was instrumental in setting aside the land at Dulles International Airport while he was Administrator of the Federal Aviation Administration. Don continued his interest when he became NASM Director and contributed many ideas to the design of the new facility. He traveled the country to meet with aviation enthusiasts, telling them about the need for the Center and soliciting their support.

The Udvar-Hazy Center features an observation tower from which visitors can watch arriving and departing Washington Dulles International Airport air traffic. The tower has been named after Admiral Engen to honor his role in securing the Center's future.

Piper J-3 Cub

First built in 1938, the Piper J-3 earned fame as a trainer and sport plane. Its success made the name "Cub" a generic term for light airplanes. The little yellow tail dragger remains one of the most recognized designs in aviation. J-3 Cubs and subsequent models are still found at fields around the world. Thousands of pilots who learned to fly in the Civilian Pilot Training Program trained in Cubs.

William T. Piper and Piper Aircraft are one of general aviation's greatest success stories. Piper took Gilbert Taylor's Tiger Kitten and E-2 designs and, with Walter Jamoneau, built the Taylor and Piper J-2, then the legendary Piper J-3. When production ended in 1947, 19,888 Piper Cubs had been built. This Cub was built in 1941 and accumulated more than 6,000 hours of flying time before being restored in 1975.

AIRCRAFT SPECIFICATIONS

Wingspan:	10.7 m (35 ft 3 in)
Length:	6.8 m (22 ft 5 in)
Height:	1.9 m (6 ft 8 in)
Weight, empty:	309 kg (680 lb)
Weight, gross:	554 kg (1,220 lb)
Top speed:	129 km/h (80 mph)
Engine:	Continental A-65, 65 hp
Manufacturer:	Piper Aircraft Corp., Lock Haven, Pa., 1941

TOP
The Piper Cub was the first aircraft to roost at the Udvar-Hazy Center. More than 300 air and spacecraft will follow.

BOTTOM
A Cub in action.

OPPOSITE
The National Air and Space Museum's Cub hung in the rafters of the Paul E. Garber Restoration Facility for many years until the Udvar-Hazy Center became a reality.

ABOVE AND RIGHT
The B-29 *Enola Gay* rested for many years in the Paul E. Garber Restoration Facility in Suitland, Maryland. Restoration took more than a decade.

BELOW
A rare look out the tail gunner's position in the B-29 *Enola Gay*—tight quarters, but an unmatched view.

Boeing B-29 Superfortress
Enola Gay

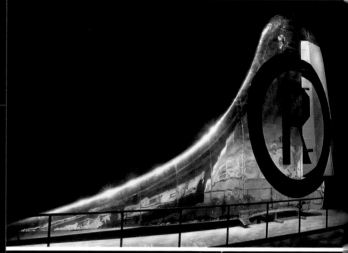

In 1995, the *Enola Gay* became the center of an exhibition controversy at the National Air and Space Museum. The tail (top), forward fuselage and one propeller (center), and cockpit sections (seen here before restoration) were part of the display.

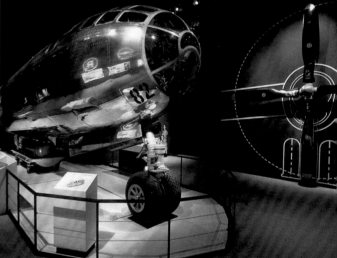

Boeing's B-29 Superfortress was the most sophisticated propeller-driven bomber of World War II, and the first bomber to house its crew in pressurized compartments. Although designed to fight in the European theater, the B-29 found its niche on the other side of the globe. In the Pacific, B-29s delivered a variety of aerial weapons: conventional bombs, incendiary bombs, mines, and two nuclear weapons.

On August 6, 1945, this Martin-built B-29-45-MO dropped the first atomic weapon used in combat on Hiroshima, Japan. Three days later, *Bockscar* (on display at the U.S. Air Force Museum near Dayton, Ohio) dropped a second atomic bomb on Nagasaki, Japan. *Enola Gay* flew as the advance weather reconnaissance aircraft that day. A third B-29, *The Great Artiste,* flew as an observation aircraft on both missions.

AIRCRAFT SPECIFICATIONS

Wingspan:	43 m (141 ft 3 in)
Length:	30.2 m (99 ft)
Height:	9 m (27 ft 9 in)
Weight, empty:	32,580 kg (71,826 lb)
Weight, gross:	63,504 kg (140,000 lb)
Top speed:	546 km/h (339 mph)
Engines:	four Wright R-3350-57 Cyclone turbo-supercharged radials, 2,200 hp
Crew:	12 (Hiroshima mission)
Armament:	two .50 caliber machine guns
Ordnance:	"Little Boy" atomic bomb
Manufacturer:	Martin Co., Omaha, Nebr., 1945

LEFT
Restoration specialist Scott Wood buffs the wing to a mirror-like finish.

BELOW
On a beautiful day in Washington, D.C., *Enola Gay* left her perch at the National Air and Space Museum in final preparation for the move to America's Hangar. Now, fully assembled, this historic aircraft is on display at the Udvar-Hazy Center.

TOP
The fuselage of a B-29 turned more than a few heads in downtown Washington, D.C., during *Enola Gay*'s trip to the Paul E. Garber Restoration Facility.

BOTTOM
In the final stages of assembly, *Enola Gay* is back together for the first time in more than 40 years.

Aichi M6A1 Seiran

Aichi chief engineer Toshio Ozaki designed the Seiran (Clear Sky Storm) during World War II to fulfill a requirement for a bomber that could operate exclusively from a submarine. Japanese war planners devised the idea as a means for striking directly at the United States mainland and other distant strategic targets, such as the Panama Canal. To support Seiran operations, the Japanese developed a special fleet of submarine aircraft carriers to bring the Seirans within striking distance.

No Seiran ever saw combat, but the Seiran-submarine weapons system represents an ingenious blend of aviation and marine technology. This M6A1 was the last airframe built and is the only surviving Seiran in the world. Allied forces discovered it in the remains of the Aichi factory after the war.

AIRCRAFT SPECIFICATIONS

Wingspan:	12.3 m (40 ft 3 in)
Length:	11.6 m (38 ft 2 in)
Height:	4.6 m (15 ft)
Weight, empty:	3,310 kg (7,282 lb)
Weight, gross:	4,445 kg (9,800 lb)
Top speed:	475 km/h (295 mph)
Engine:	Aichi AE1P Atsuta 32, 12-cylinder, liquid-cooled, inverted V, 1,400 hp
Crew:	2
Armament:	flexible rear-firing 13 mm Type-2 machine gun
Ordnance:	one 800–850-kg or two 250-kg bombs
Manufacturer:	Aichi Kokuki K. K., Eitoku, Japan, 1945

OPPOSITE TOP AND BOTTOM
Seiran's wings folded so that it fit inside a submarine.

ABOVE
Restoration specialists apply the finishing touches to
the Seiran.

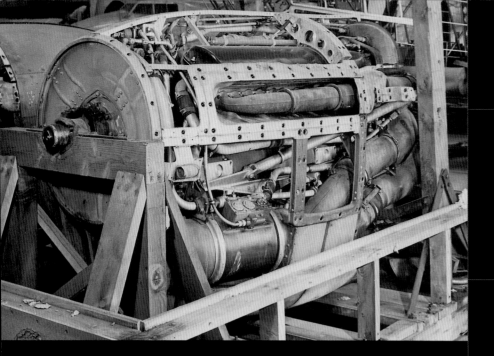

ABOVE
The powerful Allison engine was liquid cooled and a pair could deliver more than 2,800 horsepower.

BELOW
Here, the P-38 nose awaits restoration at the Paul E. Garber Restoration Facility.

Lockheed P-38
Lightning

From 1942 to 1945, U.S. Army Air Forces pilots flew the P-38 over Europe, the Mediterranean, and the Pacific; from the frozen Aleutian Islands to the sun-baked deserts of North Africa. Lockheed engineer Clarence "Kelly" Johnson and a team of designers created one of the most successful twin-engine fighters ever flown by any nation. In the Pacific Theater, Lightning pilots downed more Japanese aircraft than pilots flying any other Allied warplane.

On April 16, 1945, while at Wright Field, Ohio, for tests, Major Richard I. Bong, America's leading fighter ace, flew this aircraft. Bong had planned to fly for an hour to evaluate an experimental method of interconnecting the movement of the throttle and propeller control levers. His flight ended prematurely when his right engine exploded before he could conduct the experiment.

AIRCRAFT SPECIFICATIONS

Wingspan:	15.8 m (52 ft 0 in)
Length:	11.7 m (37 ft 10 in)
Height:	2.9 m (9 ft 10 in)
Weight, empty:	6,345 kg (14,100 lb)
Weight, gross:	7,965 kg (17,699 lb)
Engines:	two Allison V-1710-89/91, liquid-cooled in-line, 1,425 hp
Crew:	1
Armament:	one 20 mm Hispano AN-M2C cannon. Four .50 caliber Browning machine guns. External bomb load of 4,000 lbs or ten 5-in rockets
Manufacturer:	Lockheed Aircraft Corp., Burbank, Calif., November 6, 1943

ABOVE
The P-38 Lightning saw combat in every theater of operations during World War II—from Europe to the Pacific.

BELOW
The Lightning has been restored to accurately represent its World War II operational appearance.

Bell No. 2 Rocket Belt

Often called the Jet Pack, Jet Flying Belt, Jet Belt, or Jet Vest, the rocket belt is a small personal-propulsion device. Strapped on the back, it enables a person to fly short distances using low rocket power produced by a noncombusting gas.

The rocket belt concept appeared in Buck Rogers comic strips as early as 1929. Wendell Moore of Bell Aerosystems Company was the first to develop a working version in the mid-1950s. In the 1960s, the U.S. military seriously considered equipping combat soldiers with the device, but its duration of just a few seconds was too limited. A jet-powered version with longer duration was later developed, but it too proved inadequate. Today Jet Packs are used mainly in expositions, in movie stunts, in football game half-time shows, and at other events.

A pilot tests a Bell Company Rocket Belt, ascending more than a hundred feet in seconds.

Ruhrstahl X-4 Missile

The German X-4 was a small air-to-air missile of World War II that could be fired at heavily armed Allied bombers from a distance. To prevent jamming, guidance was by wires running between the missile and its launch aircraft rather than by radio. Slated for use on the Me 262 jet fighter, the X-4 could also have been fired from such piston-engine aircraft as the Ju 88, Ju 388, and Fw 190, all of which launched test missiles beginning in August 1944.

A BMW 109-548 liquid-fuel rocket engine powered the missile. Ruhrstahl produced 1,000 X-4 airframes in late 1944, but an Allied air raid destroyed the BMW engines and production lines, a blow from which the program never recovered. The Smithsonian obtained this missile from the U.S. Navy in 1948.

VEHICLE SPECIFICATIONS

Length:	2 m (6 ft 6.8 in)
Weight:	60 kg (132 lb)
Weight, warhead:	20 kg (44 lb)
Range:	5.5 km (3 mi)
Thrust:	294–1,370 N (66–309 lb)
Propellants:	Tonka 250, SV-Stoff
Manufacturer:	Ruhrstahl

Rheintochter R I Missile

The Rheintochter (Rhine Maiden) R I was an experimental German two-stage antiaircraft missile tested in the last year of World War II. Built by the Rheinmetall-Borsig company for the Luftwaffe, it was one of the largest solid-fuel rockets of the war. The R I was to be supplanted by the R III, a liquid-fuel missile with two side-mounted solid-fuel boosters that enabled it to reach a higher altitude. However, only six R IIIs were ever launched, as opposed to 82 R I missiles.

The Smithsonian acquired this Rheintochter R I from the U.S. Navy in 1969. It was displayed in the National Air and Space Museum from 1976 to the early 1980s. In 2002 it was restored to its original condition and paint scheme for exhibit at the Steven F. Udvar-Hazy Center.

VEHICLE SPECIFICATIONS

Length:	5.6 m (18 ft)
Weight:	1,100 kg (2,425 lb)
Weight, warhead:	150 kg (332 lb)
Range:	12.1 km (7.5 mi)
Thrust:	734,000 N (165,000 lb) booster, 39,144 N (8,800 lb) sustainer
Propellant:	solid diglycol rocket motor
Manufacturer:	Rheinmetall-Borsig, Germany

Hs 293 A-1 Missile

Germany developed the Hs 293 air-launched missile in World War II for use against ships or ground targets. It was basically a glide bomb assisted by a liquid-fuel rocket that fired for 10 seconds. The Hs 293 was carried under the wings or in the bomb bay of an He 111, He 177, Fw 200, or Do 217 aircraft. Its warhead was a modified SC 500 bomb containing Trialene 105 high explosive. A bombardier guided the missile by means of a joystick and radio control.

Beginning in mid-1943, Hs 293s sank several Allied ships, mostly in the Mediterranean Theater. Although Germany developed many experimental versions, only the Hs 293 A-1 was produced in quantity.

VEHICLE SPECIFICATIONS

Length:	3.6 m (11 ft 9 in)
Weight, loaded:	1,045 kg (2,304 lb)
Weight, warhead:	295 g (649 lb)
Range:	18 km (11 mi)
Thrust:	5,870 N (1,320 lb)
Propellants:	hydrogen peroxide, sodium permanganate
Manufacturer:	Henschel Flugzeugwerke

Loon Missile

Also called the JB-2 or KUW-1, the Loon was an American copy of the German pulsejet-powered V-1 "buzz bomb" of World War II. The long tube at the rear is the air-breathing pulsejet engine.

Developed late in the war, the Loon was first test launched in October 1944. Loons could be launched from the ground, ships, or aircraft, but they were never used in combat. However, U.S. Navy and Army Air Forces personnel working with Loons gained invaluable experience in handling missiles. The program was canceled in 1950, and the faster and more powerful Regulus missile replaced the Loon.

VEHICLE SPECIFICATIONS

Length:	8.2 m (27 ft)
Weight, loaded:	2,700 kg (6,000 lb)
Weight, warhead:	998 kg (2,200 lb)
Range:	242 km (150 mi)
Thrust:	2,220 N (500 lb)
Propellant:	gasoline
Manufacturer:	Ford Motor Co., Detroit, Mich.

Matador Cruise Missile

The TM-61C Matador was a U.S. Air Force turbojet-powered, surface-to-surface cruise missile of the mid-1950s to early 1960s. It could carry a conventional or nuclear warhead 1,050 kilometers (650 miles) at Mach 0.9, nearly the speed of sound, and at an altitude of up to 13 kilometers (8 miles).

The Matador was boosted from its launcher by a solid-fuel T-50 Thiokol rocket engine, which dropped off after firing. Its jet engine powered it the rest of the way to the target. The missile navigated by terrain-comparison radar or inertial guidance.

VEHICLE SPECIFICATIONS

Length:	12 m (39 ft 6 in)
Weight:	4,047 kg (8,922 lb)
Weight, warhead:	1,360 kg (3,000 lb)
Range:	1,050 km (650 mi)
Thrust:	2,087 kg (4,600 lb)
Propellant:	jet fuel
Manufacturer:	Martin Co., Baltimore, Md.

SA-2 Guideline Missile

Developed and made in the Soviet Union, the SA-2 has been used more widely than any other air defense missile in the world. In the Soviet Union it was called the Dvina; in the West it was known by its NATO code name, SA-2 Guideline (SA meaning surface-to-air). The SA-2 became operational in 1959 and was acquired by all Soviet client states. In 1960 an SA-2 downed the American U-2 spy plane piloted by Francis Gary Powers. The SA-2 was also used with deadly effect against U.S. aircraft during the war in Southeast Asia.

The SA-2 had a solid-fuel booster and a liquid-fuel second stage. Many countries made their own versions of the missile. This one, meant for export, is mounted on a transporter and required a separate launcher. SA-2s are still in use today.

VEHICLE SPECIFICATIONS

Length:	10.5 m (34 ft 6 in)
Weight, warhead:	129 kg (287 lb)
Range:	50 km (31 mi)
Propellants:	solid fuel, booster; liquid fuel, sustainer
Manufacturer:	Volkhov Defense Systems, U.S.S.R.

LEFT
Langley Aerodrome A just after leaving houseboat-mounted catapult and moments before crashing into the Potomac River on October 7, 1903.

BELOW
Langley Aerodrome A, ready for flight from its houseboat catapult launching system on the Potomac River in 1903.

ABOVE
Manly-Balzer engine used on the Langley Aerodrome A.

RIGHT
Langley Aerodrome A, being assembled on its launching platform.

Langley Aerodrome A

Samuel Langley's successful flights of model-size Aerodromes in 1896 led him to build a full-size, human-carrying airplane. Langley's simple approach was merely to scale up the unpiloted Aerodromes to human-carrying proportions, which proved to be a grave error. He focused primarily on the power plant. The completed engine, a water-cooled five-cylinder radial with remarkable power, was indeed a great achievement.

Despite the excellent engine, Langley's Aerodrome A met with disastrous results, crashing on takeoff on October 7, 1903, and again on December 8—only nine days before the Wright brothers' historic flights. While Langley blamed the launch mechanism, it is clear that the aircraft was overly complex, structurally weak, and aerodynamically unsound. The second crash ended Langley's aeronautical work.

AIRCRAFT SPECIFICATIONS

Wingspan:	14.8 m (48 ft 5 in)
Length:	16 m (52 ft 5 in)
Height:	3.5 m (11 ft 4 in)
Weight:	340 kg (750 lb) including pilot
Engine:	Manly-Balzer 5-cylinder radial, 52.4 hp
Builder:	Samuel P. Langley, Washington, D.C., 1903

TOP
The Langley Aerodrome A was rebuilt by Glenn Curtiss at Hammondsport, N.Y., in 1914. Among the many modifications made by Curtiss were new wings, the addition of floats, replacing the engine with a Curtiss V-8, and Curtiss-style controls. In this image, Curtiss Company pilot, Walter Johnson, flies the highly modified Langley Aerodrome A in 1914.

BOTTOM
The Langley Aerodrome A on exhibit in the Smithsonian's Arts and Industries Building after restoration to its original 1903 configuration by the Smithsonian in 1918.

LEFT
This F-4 served as a U.S. Navy fighter during the Vietnam War but later, after it was modified and improved, was transferred to the U.S. Marine Corps.

BELOW
Graphic artist Jim Qualls has created this portrait of NASM's F-4S Phantom II in its Navy colors.

McDonnell F-4S Phantom II

The U.S. Air Force, Navy, and Marine Corps and air forces of 12 other nations have flown the multi-role Phantom II. In this aircraft, then a Navy F-4J, on May 18, 1972, Cmdr. S. C. Flynn and his radar intercept officer, Lt. W. H. John, spotted three enemy MiG fighters off the coast of Vietnam and shot down one MiG-21 with a Sidewinder air-to-air missile. This Phantom also flew combat air patrols and bombing missions during the Linebacker II bombing campaign that same year.

Later assigned to the Marine Corps, this F-4J was extensively modernized and designated an F-4S. Changes included improving the engines (smokeless), hydraulics, electronics, and wiring; modifying the wings to increase maneuverability; and adding a radar homing and warning antenna, as well as formation tape lights on the fuselage and vertical tail.

AIRCRAFT SPECIFICATIONS

Wingspan:	11.6 m (38 ft 5 in)
Length:	17.7 m (58 ft 3 in)
Height:	5 m (17 ft 4 in)
Weight, empty:	13,960 kg (30,780 lb)
Weight, gross:	23,250 kg (51,300 lb)
Top speed:	2,298 km/h (1,428 mph), Mach 2.2
Engines:	two General Electric J79-GE-10 turbojets, 8,119 kg (17,900 lb) thrust
Crew:	2
Ordnance:	four AIM-7 Sparrow and four AIM-9 Sidewinder air-to-air missiles, 7,257-kg (16,000-lb) bomb load
Manufacturer:	McDonnell Douglas Corp., St. Louis, Mo., 1970

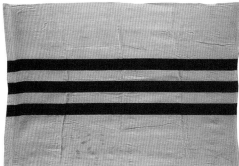

Flag of the Republic of Vietnam.

Both of these flags from the Vietnam War are part of the NASM collection.

Flag of the Viet Cong (People's Liberation Forces in South Vietnam).

LEFT
The F-4, still a "J" model, lands on the USS Saratoga.

Apollo Extravehicular Gloves
These gloves were developmental versions
of those later worn on the lunar surface.

Lunar EVA Artifacts

THESE OBJECTS ARE EXAMPLES of personal equipment and tools issued to astronauts of the Mercury, Gemini, and Apollo programs. Some of the objects were used in training for missions, others during the actual missions. They include items of protective clothing (gloves, helmets, and boots), a spacesuit worn on the Moon, and examples of the types of tools astronauts used on the lunar surface. The actual tools used on the Moon were left behind.

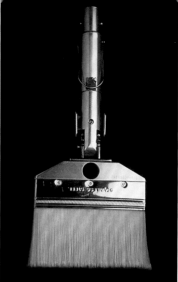

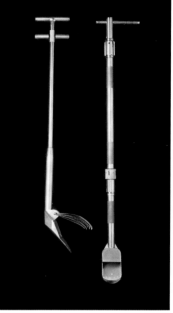

OPPOSITE MIDDLE
Earth

OPPOSITE BOTTOM
Apollo 17 Harrison Schmitt next to large boulder.

TOP
Astronaut Charles Duke collecting lunar samples at Station 1.

BOTTOM
Astronaut James Irwin beside the Lunar Rover.

RIGHT
Seen here are examples of tools used on the lunar surface during the Apollo Program: (top) lunar brush; (middle) scongs—a combined scoop and tongs device—and a small scoop; (bottom) trenching tool.

Balloonamania

THE BROTHERS JOSEPH AND ETIENNE Montgolfier sent their first balloon aloft from the town square of Annonay, France, on June 4, 1783. It was a simple paper and fabric bag, 11 meters (35 feet) in diameter, filled with hot air. The event marked the beginning of a decade of great hot air and gas balloon flights in Europe and America.

The knowledge that human beings had actually taken to the sky after centuries of dreaming generated great popular excitement. "The novelty of the thing is so great," an American visitor to Paris remarked, "that it engrosses half the talk and attention of the city." Benjamin Franklin agreed. "All the conversation here at present turns upon the Balloons," he said to a friend, "and the means of managing them so as to give Men the Advantage of Flying."

The Balloon and Popular Culture
The balloon had an immediate impact on popular culture. Beverages and dances commemorated this wonder of the age. Clothing and hat styles were inspired by the colorful craft rising above the rooftops of Paris and London.

Balloon motifs decorated items of furniture, jewelry, ceramics, boxes, wallpaper, fans, upholstery fabric, and dozens of other items. The objects in this display case, dating from 1783 through the twentieth century, illustrate the continuing popularity of decorative themes involving balloons and airships.

TOP TO BOTTOM
Angoulême porcelain cup
Shagreen diptych case
French fan leaf
Jewel coffret with balloon decoration

RIGHT
Acajou Louis XVI poudreuse

OPPOSITE
Acajou Louis XVI secrétaire abattant

ABOVE
Angoulême porcelain saucer
Angoulême porcelain cup

LEFT
Walnut chair

1783

June 4: Joseph and Etienne Montgolfier, sons of a paper manufacturer from Annonay, France, fly a small balloon in public for the first time.

Aug. 27: J. A. C. Charles flies the first small hydrogen-filled balloon from the Champ de Mars, a cavalry parade ground in the heart of Paris.

Sept. 19: The Montgolfier brothers send the first living creatures aloft from the palace at Versailles, outside Paris. The sheep, rooster, and duck return safely to earth a few minutes later.

Nov. 21: Pilâtre de Rozier and the Marquis d'Arlandes become the first human beings to make a free flight aboard a Montgolfier hot air balloon.

Nov. 25: Francesco Zambecarri, an Italian living in London, launches the first small unmanned balloon in England.

Dec. 1: J. A. C. Charles and M. N. Robert make the first flight aboard a hydrogen-filled balloon.

1784

Feb. 25: Italian aeronaut Paolo Andreani makes the first balloon flight outside of France.

June 24: Peter Carnes, a lawyer and tavern keeper from Bladensburg, Maryland, sends the first American aloft on a tethered balloon flight, a 13-year-old Baltimore lad named Edward Warren.

Sept. 15: Vincenzo Lunardi, secretary to the Neapolitan ambassador, makes the first free flight from London.

1785

Jan. 7: J. P. F. Blanchard, a French aeronaut, and Dr. John Jeffries, an American loyalist living in England, make the first flight across the English Channel.

1793

Jan. 9: J. P. F. Blanchard makes the first free flight from American soil, traveling from Philadelphia to Deptford Township, New Jersey.

ABOVE
Louis XVI commode

BELOW
Gold-tooled red leather scent bottle case

RIGHT
Louis XVI carved gift gesso and wood wall mirror

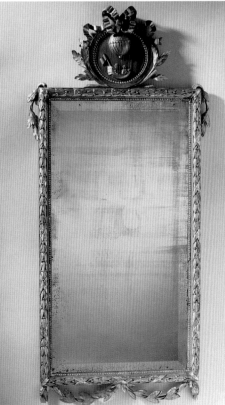

Boeing 367-80 "Dash 80"

Purchased first as a refueling plane for the U.S. Air Force, the Boeing 707 became one of the most successful airliners ever built.

U.S. civil aviation entered the jet age on July 15, 1954, when the Boeing 367-80, or "Dash 80," first took flight. Designed for the U.S. Air Force as a jet tanker-transport, this airplane was the prototype for America's first commercial jet airliner, the Boeing 707.

Boeing began designing the Dash 80 without a contract in 1952. In 1954 the Air Force purchased the first of 820 KC-135 tankers, as the modified version was designated. At Pan American's request, Boeing widened the fuselage to accommodate six-across seating for airline use. This larger aircraft became the Boeing 707, of which 855 were built between 1957 and 1992. The Dash 80 tested many new technologies, including new engines and engine nacelles, different wing shapes, and a variety of flaps and control surfaces, before it was donated to the Smithsonian in 1972. Boeing restored it in 1995.

AIRCRAFT SPECIFICATIONS

Wingspan:	39.4 m (129 ft 8 in)
Length:	39 m (127 ft 10 in)
Height:	11.6 m (38 ft)
Weight, empty:	41,786 kg (92,120 lb)
Weight, gross:	86,184 kg (190,000 lb)
Top speed:	937 km/h (582 mph)
Engines:	four Pratt and Whitney JT3D, 7,711 kg (17,000 lb) thrust
Manufacturer:	Boeing Aircraft Co., Seattle, Wash., 1954

Boeing 307 Stratoliner
Clipper Flying Cloud

First flown in late 1938, the Boeing 307 was the first airliner with a pressurized fuselage. It could carry 33 passengers in great comfort and cruise at 6,096 meters (20,000 feet), while maintaining a cabin pressure of 2,438 meters (8,000 feet). This enabled the Stratoliner to fly above most bad weather, thereby providing a faster and smoother ride.

The Stratoliner incorporated the wings, tail, and engines of the Boeing B-17C bomber. The wide fuselage was fitted with sleeper berths and reclining seats. Ten Stratoliners were built. The prototype was lost in an accident, but five were delivered to TWA and three were purchased by Pan American Airways. TWA owner Howard Hughes purchased a heavily modified version for his personal use. The airplane displayed here was flown by Pan American as the *Clipper Flying Cloud.* Boeing restored it in 2001.

AIRCRAFT SPECIFICATIONS

Wingspan:	32.7 m (107 ft 3 in)
Length:	22.7 m (74 ft 4 in)
Height:	6.3 m (20 ft 9 in)
Weight, empty:	13,749 kg (30,310 lb)
Weight, gross:	19,051 kg (42,000 lb)
Top speed:	396 km/h (246 mph)
Engines:	four Wright GR-1820 Cyclones, 900 hp
Manufacturer:	Boeing Aircraft Co., Seattle, Wash., 1940

TOP TO BOTTOM

The sleek silver appearance marked the Stratoliner as a luxurious tranport. Interior ammenities were much more comfortable than most commercial airliners today.

The Stratoliner displays the American flag at one of many airshows visited over the years.

Pitts Special S-1C
Little Stinker

The oldest surviving Pitts Special, *Little Stinker* was the second aircraft constructed by Curtis Pitts. Pitts introduced the S-1 in 1945, the first of a famous line that dominated aerobatic competition throughout the 1960s and 1970s because of their small size, light weight, short wingspan, and extreme agility. Subsequent models still fly in all aerobatic categories and are standard aircraft for advanced aerobatic training.

Betty Skelton bought this airplane in 1948, and with it she won the 1949 and 1950 International Feminine Aerobatic Championships. Her impressive flying skill and public relations ability heightened awareness of both aerobatics and the Pitts design. Skelton sold *Little Stinker* in 1951, but she and her husband later reacquired it and donated it to the Smithsonian. A volunteer crew restored it from 1996 to 2001.

TOP TO BOTTOM

Betty Skelton had this brilliant red and white sunburst scheme painted onto the Pitts S-1C after she won her second Feminine Aerobatic Champion title.

A passing pilot snapped this photograph of Skelton while she was flying over Florida.

This dedicated volunteer crew restored *Little Stinker* over a six-year period at the Paul E. Garber Restoration Facility. Left to right: George Rousseau, Roger Guest, Joe Fichera, and Cindy Rousseau.

The *Little Stinker*, resplendent in its new fabric and paint, sparkles in the sun at its rollout. Pitts Specials are still popular aerobatic and training aircraft.

AIRCRAFT SPECIFICATIONS

Wingspan:	4.9 m (16 ft 10 in)
Length:	4.4 m (14 ft 6 in)
Height:	1.7 m (5 ft 6 in)
Weight:	257 kg (568 lb)
Top speed:	257 km/h (160 mph)
Engine:	Continental C85-8FJ, 85 hp
Builder:	Curtis Pitts, 1946

The Laser 200 was the first aircraft to be suspended at the Udvar-Hazy Center.

BELOW
Leo Loudenslager's helmet and flightsuit are displayed in the Aerobatic Case along with flight clothing from famed aerobatic pilots Bob Hoover, Patty Wagstaff, and Suzanne Oliver.

Loudenslager Laser 200

With the Laser 200, Leo Loudenslager won an unprecedented seven U.S. National Aerobatic Champion titles between 1975 and 1982, as well as the 1980 World Champion title. The airplane originated as a Stephens Akro, a sleek aerobatic design, but by 1975 Loudenslager had completely modified the airplane with a new forward fuselage, wings, tail, and cockpit. The Laser 200 proved lighter, stronger, and more powerful, enabling Loudenslager to perform sharper and more difficult maneuvers.

Loudenslager's legacy is evident in the tumbling and twisting but precise routines flown by current champions and air show pilots. The Laser 200 heavily influenced the look and performance of the next generation of aerobatic aircraft, including the Extra, which dominated competition throughout the 1990s.

AIRCRAFT SPECIFICATIONS

Wingspan:	8 m (26 ft 2 in)
Length:	5.5 m (18 ft 8 in)
Height:	1.6 m (5 ft 5 in)
Weight:	400 kg (885 lb)
Top speed:	370 km/h (230 mph)
Engine:	Lycoming IO-360-A1A, 200 hp
Builder:	Leo Loudenslager, 1971

Concorde

The first supersonic airliner to enter service, the Concorde flew thousands of passengers across the Atlantic at twice the speed of sound for over 25 years. Designed and built by Aérospatiale of France and the British Aircraft Corporation, the graceful Concorde was a stunning technological achievement that could not overcome serious economic problems.

In 1976, Air France and British Airways jointly inaugurated Concorde service to destinations around the globe. Carrying up to 100 passengers in great comfort, the Concorde catered to first-class passengers for whom speed was critical. It could cross the Atlantic in fewer than four hours—half the time of a conventional jet airliner. However, its high operating costs resulted in very high fares that limited the number of passengers who could afford to fly it. These problems and a shrinking market eventually forced the reduction of service until all Concordes were retired in 2003.

In 1989, Air France signed a letter of agreement to donate a Concorde to the National Air and Space Museum upon the aircraft's retirement. On June 12, 2003, Air France honored that agreement, donating Concorde F-BVFA to the Museum upon the completion of its last flight. This aircraft was the first Air France Concorde to open service to Rio de Janeiro, Washington, D.C., and New York and (upon retirement) had flown 17,824 hours.

AIRCRAFT SPECIFICATIONS

Wingspan:	25.56 m (83 ft 10 in)
Length:	61.66 m (202 ft 3 in)
Height:	11.3 m (37 ft 1 in)
Weight, empty:	79,265 kg (174,750 lb)
Weight, gross:	181,435 kg (400,000 lb)
Top speed:	2,179 km/h (1,350 mph)
Engines:	Four Rolls-Royce/SNECMA Olympus 593 Mk 602, 17,259 kg (38,050 lb) thrust each
Manufacturer:	Société Nationale Industrielle Aérospatiale, Paris, France, and British Aircraft Corporation, London, United Kingdom

The majestic Concorde touches down for the final time at
Dulles International Airport. The towering tail will be easy
to locate from any location on the Udvar-Hazy Center floor.

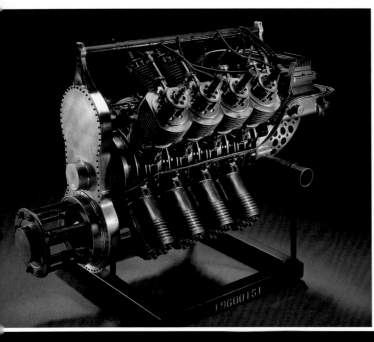

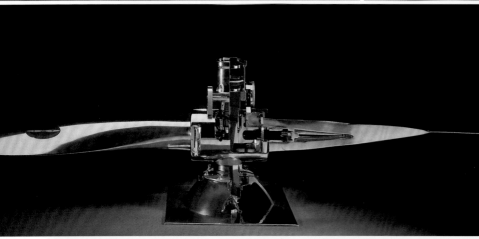

Aircraft Propulsion

ON THE MORNING of December 17, 1903, the first aeronautical propulsion system—a gas engine, propellers, and the equipment needed to make them operate—took to the air in the Wright *Flyer*. The aeronautical community continued to refine that system for heavier-than-air flight until the introduction of the gas turbine engine in the 1940s revolutionized the design and use of aircraft.

The objects displayed here at Udvar-Hazy include reciprocating internal combustion and gas turbine engines as well as the components and support technologies that make up aeronautical propulsion systems. These artifacts reveal the multiple approaches to improving the performance of aeronautical propulsion technology during the twentieth century.

OPPOSITE TOP LEFT
Taft-Peirce V-8 engine, 1911

OPPOSITE TOP RIGHT
General Electric Type C-series Turbosupercharger Cutaway, World War II

OPPOSITE CENTER LEFT
Hamilton Standard Controllable-Pitch Propeller Cutaway, 1933

OPPOSITE CENTER RIGHT
Engine cylinders, 1903–1950

OPPOSITE BOTTOM
Before and after restoration Lycoming XR-7755-3 Radial 36, 1945

RIGHT TOP TO BOTTOM
Manufacturer's employee badges, 1920–1945

Pratt & Whitney R-1340 Wasp tools and toolbox, 1927

TOP
The Fa 330 at the Paul E. Garber Restoration Facility's shop in 1975 prior to restoration.

ABOVE LEFT
The restored aircraft is readied for shipment to the NASM mall location for display.

RIGHT
The Fa 330 underwent its initial submarine trials aboard *U523* in the Baltic Sea during August 1942.

Focke-Achgelis Fa 330

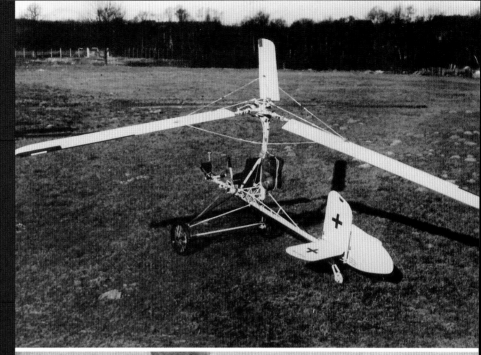

This rotary-wing kite enabled World War II German submarines to locate targets in heavy seas. Simple to fly, the Fa 330 could be towed aloft as high as 220 meters (722 feet), where the pilot could sight as far as 53 kilometers (33 miles). He communicated his observations by a telephone line that ran along the tow cable. An ingenious parachute system allowed the pilot to escape from the aircraft at relatively low altitudes.

A crew of four could assemble or disassemble an Fa 330 in three minutes. When not in use, it remained stowed in two watertight tubes in the U-boat's conning tower. U-boat commanders disliked the aircraft—it gave away their submarine's location both visually and on radar. Only Type IX D2 U-boats operating in the Indian Ocean deployed them.

AIRCRAFT SPECIFICATIONS

Rotor diameter:	8.5 m (28 ft)
Length:	4.5 m (14 ft 8 in)
Height:	1.7 m (5 ft 6 in)
Weight, empty:	75 kg (165 lb)
Weight, gross:	175 kg (386 lb)
Top speed:	80 km/h (50 mph)
Manufacturer:	Weser Flugzeugbau, Hoykenkamp, Germany, 1944

TOP
Fa 330s were at times equipped with wheels for training U-Boat crewmen.

BOTTOM
A close-up of the small instrument panel that was located between the pilot's feet.

Rollout of the completed NASM Nieuport 28 on August 14, 2000. An assemblage of components of at least five different Nieuport 28s, it was finished in the markings of Lt. James A. Meissner of the U.S. Air Service's famous "Hat-in-the-Ring" 94th Aero Squadron.

ABOVE LEFT
The 95th Aero Squadron's Nieuport 28s at Gengoult Aerodrome, Toul, France, 1918.

ABOVE RIGHT
Nieuport 28 (serial #6298) at McCook Field, Dayton, Ohio, in 1918.

RIGHT
Nieuport 28s were susceptible to engine fires.

OPPOSITE TOP TO BOTTOM
Lineup of Nieuport 28s during the making of the Hollywood film *The Dawn Patrol* in 1938. Film stars Errol Flynn and David Niven are in the first two aircraft.

The NASM's Nieuport 28 was flown by airshow performer and founder of the Old Rhinebeck Aerodrome Museum, Cole Palen, from 1959 to 1972. Shown here at a Rhinebeck airshow in the mid-1960s, Palen traded the airplane to the NASM in 1986.

Lt. James A. Meissner of the U.S. Air Service's famous "Hat-in-the-Ring" 94th Aero Squadron, wearing his newly awarded Croix de Guerre, May 15, 1918. NASM's Nieuport 28 was finished in the colors of Meissner's aircraft.

Nieuport 28C.1

The Nieuport 28C.1 was introduced in mid-1917 but was rejected by France in favor of the sturdier, more advanced SPAD XIII. With no suitable fighter of its own, the United States adopted the Nieuport until France could provide the much-in-demand SPADs. Nieuport 28s were the first aircraft to serve with an American fighter unit under U.S. command and in support of U.S. troops, and the first to score a victory with a U.S. unit.

The Nieuport 28 also made its mark after the war. The U.S. Navy used 12 for shipboard launching trials in 1919–21. The U.S. Army operated others in the 1920s. Several in private hands were modified for air racing, and some found their way into Hollywood movies. Still others became privately owned and flew in sporting and commercial capacities. This airplane contains components from as many as five Nieuport 28s.

AIRCRAFT SPECIFICATIONS

Wingspan:	8.2 m (26 ft 11 in)
Length:	6.5 m (21 ft 4 in)
Height:	2.5 m (8 ft 2 in)
Weight, empty:	533 kg (1,173 lb)
Weight, gross:	737 kg (1,625 lb)
Top speed:	200 km/h (124 mph)
Engine:	Gnôme Monosoupape 9N rotary, 160 hp
Armament:	two .30 cal. Vickers aircraft machine guns
Manufacturer:	Société Anonyme des Établissements Nieuport, Issy-les-Moulineaux, France, 1918

Lear Jet Model 23

The first Lear Jets, the Model 23 Continentals, were the first products of the original Lear Jet Corporation for the new field of business and personal jet aviation. So significant was the design that for years "Lear Jet" was synonymous with "bizjet." William P. Lear Sr. initiated the Lear Jet's development in 1959. The aircraft drew upon the structural quality of the Swiss AFA P-16 strike-fighter and featured a fuselage that narrowed at each side where the wing and engine nacelles extended outward—a design concept known as "area rule"—to provide smooth airflow around the engines.

Successive Lear Jet models set many speed records. The Lear Jet line is now part of the Bombardier Aerospace family, which includes Challenger and Global Express aircraft. This is the second Lear Jet built and the first production Model 23. Lear Jet used it as a test aircraft.

AIRCRAFT SPECIFICATIONS

Wingspan:	10.8 m (35 ft 7 in)
Length:	13.2 m (43 ft 3 in)
Height:	3.8 m (12 ft 7 in)
Weight, empty:	2,790 kg (6,150 lb)
Weight, gross:	5,783 kg (12,750 lb)
Top speed:	903 km/h (561 mph)
Engines:	two General Electric CJ 610-1 turbojets, 1,293 kg (2,850 lb) thrust
Manufacturer:	Lear Jet Corp., Wichita, Kans., 1964

TOP TO BOTTOM
Lear Jets easily cruised above the clouds and most airliners, providing a smooth and speedy flight.

NASA and other government agencies flew Lear Jets as business aircraft, shown here, but NASA used the second Lear Jet, N802L, as a wind tunnel model.

Dassault Falcon 20

Wendy, FedEx's first aircraft, started the overnight air express industy on April 17, 1973.

Flying this Dassault Falcon 20, Federal Express revolutionized the air express industry in 1973 when it pioneered the overnight delivery of high-priority packages. FedEx purchased 33 of the popular French Dassault Falcon 20 business jets as its first aircraft, modifying each with a cargo door and a strengthened floor. The Falcon was fast and reliable, had an excellent payload for its size, and could reach any point in the United States from the company's Memphis, Tennessee, hub. This airplane, Federal Express's first, was named *Wendy,* after the daughter of FedEx founder Frederick W. Smith. FedEx donated it to the Smithsonian in 1983.

Derived from the Mystère IV fighter, the Falcon was originally designed to carry 10 passengers. Almost 500 airplanes were produced from 1963 through 1983.

AIRCRAFT SPECIFICATIONS

Wingspan:	16.3 m (53 ft 6 in)
Length:	17.2 m (56 ft 4 in)
Height:	5.7 m (17 ft 7 in)
Weight, empty:	7,230 kg (15,940 lb)
Weight, gross:	13,000 kg (28,660 lb)
Top speed:	862 km/h (535 mph)
Engines:	two General Electric CF700-2D turbofans, 1,983 kg (4,315 lb) thrust
Manufacturer:	Avions Marcel Dassault/Breguet Aviation, Paris, France, 1973

Lockheed SR-71A Blackbird

ABOVE
After flying from Los Angeles to Washington, D.C., in 1 hour and 4 minutes, this SR-71 landed at Dulles International Airport and was transferred to the nation's aircraft collection.

BELOW
The Blackbird was built for speed—Mach 3 plus. It was the Corvette of modern aircraft and is still the fastest aircraft ever built.

RIGHT (BACKGROUND)
Captain "Buck" Adams gives a spirited thumbs-up before departing with his RSO, Major William "Bill" Machorek, from London on another Blackbird record-setting flight. On September 13, 1974, this SR-71 flew from London to Los Angeles in about 4 hours.

No reconnaissance aircraft in history has operated globally in more hostile airspace or with such complete impunity than the SR-71, the world's fastest jet-propelled aircraft. The Blackbird's performance and operational achievements placed it at the pinnacle of aviation technology developments during the Cold War.

This Blackbird accrued about 2,800 hours of flight time during 24 years of active service with the U.S. Air Force. On its last flight, March 6, 1990, Lt. Col. Ed Yielding and Lt. Col. Joseph Vida set a speed record by flying from Los Angeles to Washington, D.C., in 1 hour, 4 minutes, 20 seconds, averaging 3,418 kilometers (2,124 miles) per hour. At the flight's conclusion, they landed at Washington Dulles International Airport and turned the airplane over to the Smithsonian.

AIRCRAFT SPECIFICATIONS

Wingspan:	16.9 m (55 ft 7 in)
Length:	32.7 m (107 ft 5 in)
Height:	5.6 m (18 ft 6 in)
Weight, empty:	27,216 kg (60,000 lb)
Weight, gross:	63,504 kg (140,000 lb)
Top speed:	3,620 km/h (2,250 mph), Mach 3.3
Engines:	two Pratt & Whitney J-58 (JT11D-20B), 15,422 kg (34,000 lb) thrust
Crew:	2
Manufacturer:	Lockheed Aircraft Corp., Palmdale, Calif., 1967

The Blackbird's cockpit was a tight fit for the crew, who wore bulky pressure suits during each mission.

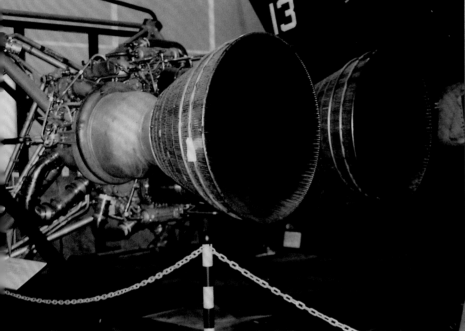

Rocket Engines

LEFT TOP TO BOTTOM

REDSTONE ROCKET ENGINE

The Redstone rocket engine was the United States' first operational large-scale rocket engine. Development began in 1950, and on January 31, 1958, a modified Redstone rocket called a Jupiter-C launched Explorer 1, the first successful U.S. satellite, into orbit. On May 5, 1961, a Redstone launched Alan B. Shepard, the first American astronaut to enter space. The Redstone was the forerunner of other important large-scale engines, including the main engine for the Space Shuttle.

TITAN I ROCKET ENGINE

The Titan I XLR-87 rocket engine powered the first stage of the two-stage Titan I intercontinental ballistic missile (ICBM). The engine consists of two side-by-side rocket chambers; the missile's second stage was a one-chamber, lower-thrust engine. Both first- and second-stage engines burned liquid oxygen and kerosene.

Developed beginning in 1954 as a backup to the Atlas ICBM, the Titan I was intended to help close the "missile gap" with the Soviet Union during the Cold War. It was later replaced by the improved Titan II, which had storable fuels and could be prepared for launch faster. The Titan II also launched the two-man Project Gemini spacecraft.

JUPITER S-3 ROCKET ENGINE

A modification of the Redstone engine, the S-3 powered the Jupiter missile, the first U.S. intermediate-range ballistic missile. Rocketdyne began developing the Jupiter engine in 1956. The Jupiter missile was used until 1963, and a modified version with additional upper stages, called the Juno II, was developed to launch spacecraft. Junos launched two Pioneer unmanned lunar probes in the late 1950s and put the Explorer 7, 8, and 11 satellites into Earth orbit.

OPPOSITE TOP LEFT

NAVAHO ROCKET ENGINE

A two-chambered, liquid-fuel rocket engine served as the booster for the Navaho missile, which was powered by two ramjets. The huge, vertically launched intercontinental cruise missile was designed to strike a target up to 8,850 kilometers (5,500 miles) away. The Navaho never became operational. Its unsuccessful testing program and enormous development cost, which had reached almost a billion dollars, caused the program to be canceled in 1957.

However, the Navaho was an important stage in the evolution of American large-scale liquid-fuel engines, including those for the Redstone, Jupiter, Thor, and Atlas missiles, the Saturn V Apollo launch vehicle, and the Space Shuttle.

OPPOSITE TOP RIGHT

V-2 ROCKET ENGINE

North American Aviation built this copy of a World War II German V-2 rocket engine around 1948 to give its engineers experience in the design and manufacture of large liquid-fuel rocket engines. One of six built, it was never fired in tests, but it led to greatly improved rocket engines and the founding of North American's Rocketdyne Division. Rocketdyne later developed engines for the Redstone, Atlas, Thor, and Jupiter missiles, as well as the Saturn V Apollo launch vehicle and the Space Shuttle.

OPPOSITE BOTTOM

GODDARD 1935 A-SERIES ROCKET

This is probably the liquid-fuel rocket Robert H. Goddard tried to launch on September 23, 1935, at his facility near Roswell, New Mexico. He attempted to demonstrate its capabilities to supporters Charles Lindbergh and Harry Guggenheim. The Guggenheim Foundation for the Promotion of Aeronautics funded Goddard's experiments in New Mexico.

A technical problem prevented the flight. But because earlier A-series rocket launches had succeeded, both Lindbergh and Guggenheim felt Goddard was on the right track. Lindbergh persuaded Goddard to donate a complete A-series rocket to the Smithsonian, which he did in November 1935.

Mobile Quarantine
Facility (Apollo 11)

This Mobile Quarantine Facility (MQF) was one of four
built by NASA for astronauts returning from the Moon.
Its purpose was to prevent the unlikely spread of lunar
contagions by isolating the astronauts from contact with
other people. A converted Airstream trailer, the MQF
contained living and sleeping quarters, a kitchen, and
a bathroom. Quarantine was assured by keeping the air
pressure inside lower than the pressure outside and by
filtering the air vented from the facility.

This MQF was used by Apollo 11 astronauts Armstrong,
Aldrin, and Collins immediately after their return to Earth.
They remained in it for 65 hours, while the MQF was flown
from the aircraft carrier *Hornet* to a quarantine facility at
the Johnson Space Center in Houston. They were allowed
to emerge once scientists were sure they were not infected
with "moon germs."

TOP LEFT
After splashdown, the astronauts don protective suits and then head for quarantine in the MQF.

TOP RIGHT
Apollo 11 crew inside the MQF, Astronaut Michael Collins (left), the command module pilot, became the first Director of the National Air and Space Museum.

BOTTOM LEFT
First visits with family were through the large glass picture window of the MQF. Here, Mrs. Armstrong, Aldrin, and Collins visit the Apollo 11 crew.

BOTTOM RIGHT
President Richard M. Nixon welcomes the crew after their historic journey to the Moon.

OPPOSITE TOP TO BOTTOM
Apollo 11 astronaut Buzz Aldrin near the American flag on the moon's surface.

Neil Armstrong, the first man to set foot on the moon, and Aldrin were monitored by a camera high atop the Lunar Excursion Module (LEM).

The Mobile Quarantine Facility (MQF) was carried on the aircraft carrier USS *Hornet*.

HORNET + 3

TOP

This "short snorter" signed by many military aviation notables, Hap Arnold and Jimmy Doolittle to name a few, was carried by aviators who had flown across the vast reaches of ocean to frequently remote locations.

BELOW LEFT AND RIGHT

Nazi Swastika

Taken as a war trophy, this Nazi symbol—the swastika—was cut from a German glider.

Japanese Flag

It was tradition for the family of any Japanese citizen who was called to service to write messages of encouragement on a flag or sash that would be carried into battle for luck and protection.

Small Artifacts

THROUGHOUT AMERICA'S HANGAR there are displayed more than just air and spacecraft. Significant artifacts representing the history of aviation fill a number of exhibit cases related to a variety of topics—from sport aviation to the most modern military advances yet witnessed. Objects representing not only America's aviation experiences but also many spectacular fragments of history from around the globe help to expose some of the personal side of a very technologically oriented subject. The NASM small artifact collection contains more than 50,000 objects.

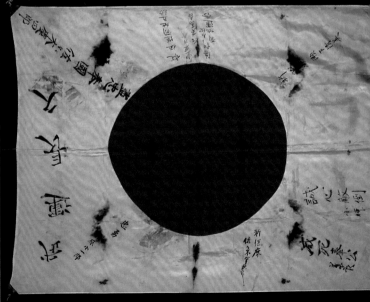

OPPOSITE TOP LEFT

General Curtis E. LeMay's service cap.

OPPOSITE TOP RIGHT

Several World War II leather jackets are on display featuring traditional artwork. Behind these jackets is General Hap Arnold's 5-star flag. Arnold directed that one of each type of WWII aircraft be preserved for all time. The richness of the NASM military collection has its roots in Arnold's orders.

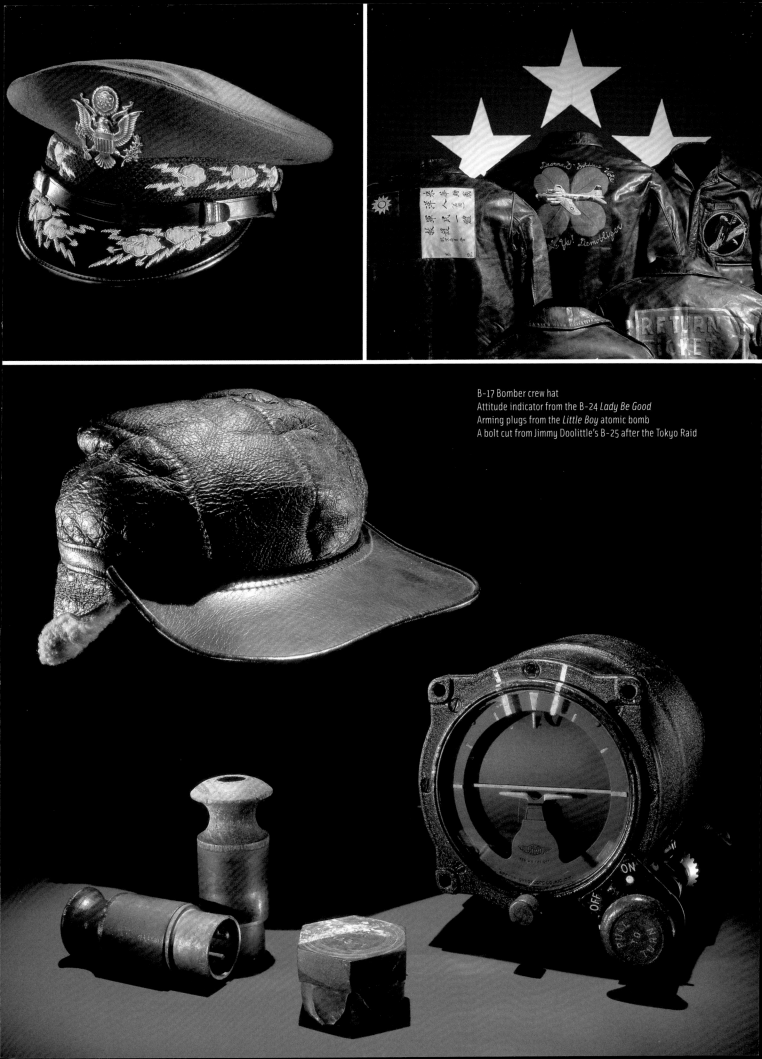

B-17 Bomber crew hat
Attitude indicator from the B-24 *Lady Be Good*
Arming plugs from the *Little Boy* atomic bomb
A bolt cut from Jimmy Doolittle's B-25 after the Tokyo Raid

TOP LEFT
Medals earned by Lafayette Escadrille pilot Edwin C. Parsons.

TOP RIGHT
World War I shell casing brass artwork.

BOTTOM LEFT
Artifacts from the 9/11 attacks on the World Trade Center and the Pentagon.

BOTTOM RIGHT
A North Vietnamese rocket launcher
Viet Cong sandals
"Dog Doo" transmitter used by the CIA to monitor movement on the Ho Chi Minh trail

Reconnaissance Party Suits

(left) Worn by an RF-4C pilot, this "Rhino" driver (another name for any F-4 crewman) trained for low altitude tactical missions throughout the Pacific during the Cold War.

(right) Worn by an SR-71 Pilot, the HABU patch indicates that this pilot has flown operational strategic reconnaissance missions.

Lockheed Martin X-35B STOVL Joint Strike Fighter

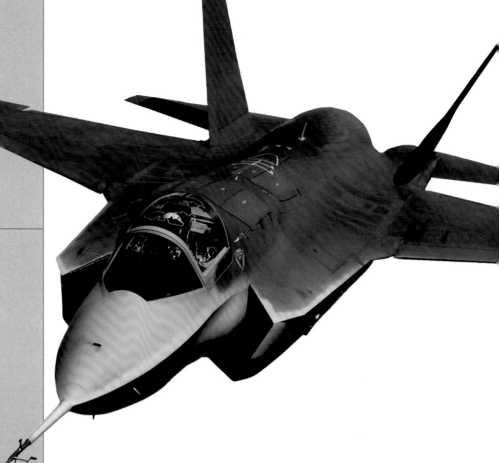

The Joint Strike Fighter is a stealthy, supersonic, multi-role fighter. Three versions are planned. The conventional takeoff and landing variant, designed for the U.S. Air Force, will be built in the largest quantities. The U.S. Navy's carrier variant features larger wing and control surfaces, additional wingtip ailerons, and a special structure to absorb punishing catapult launches and arrested landings. The short takeoff/vertical landing version has a unique shaft-driven, lift-fan propulsion system that enables the aircraft to take off from a very short runway or small aircraft carrier and land vertically.

This first X-35 ever built was modified to include the lift-fan engine. It was the first aircraft in history to achieve a short takeoff, level supersonic dash, and vertical landing in a single flight, and the first to fly using the shaft-driven, lift-fan propulsion system.

ABOVE
The X-35 test program was one of the shortest and most successful in aviation history. The X-35B will replace the AV-8B Harrier, among other aging jet platforms. It will be flown by the U.S. Marine Corps and the air forces of Great Britain.

BELOW
The X-35C, designed specifically for the U.S. Navy and carrier operations, has larger wings and stronger landing gear. It has been retired and is displayed at PAX River, where it was flight tested. The NASM aircraft was the original X-35A designed for the U.S. Air Force and was modified as the X-35B after successful completion of the initial testing phase.

AIRCRAFT SPECIFICATIONS

Wingspan:	10 m (33 ft)
Length:	15.47 m (50 ft 9 in)
Height:	5 m (15 ft)
Weight:	15,876 kg (35,000 lb)
Engine:	one Pratt & Whitney JSF119-PW-611 turbofan, total vertical lift 164.6 kN (37,000 lb)
Crew:	1
Armament:	internal cannon
Ordnance:	two AIM-120 air-to-air missiles and two 1,000-lb precision-guided bombs
Manufacturer:	Lockheed Martin, Palmdale, Calif., 2001

The NASM X-35B STOVL was the first aircraft in history to accomplish a short takeoff, supersonic run, and vertical landing on the same mission—the Hat Trick.

Testing the Pratt & Whitney JSF119-PW-611 turbofan on the engine test stand at night provided some spectacular views.

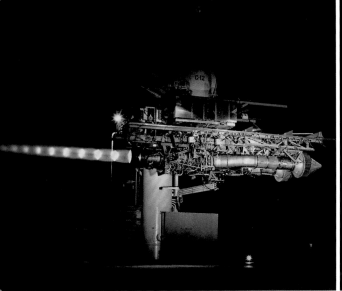

Caudron G.4

Although World War I fighter aircraft often command greater attention, the most influential role of aviation in the war was reconnaissance. An early light bomber and reconnaissance aircraft, the French Caudron G.4 was a principal type used when these critical air power roles were being conceived and pioneered.

The extensive deployment of the Caudron G.4 for reconnaissance during World War I makes it an especially important early military aircraft. Despite its speed and armament limitations, the G.4 was quite reliable, had a good rate of climb, and was pleasant to fly—characteristics that also made it a good training aircraft. Many Allied pilots received their initial flight training in G.4s. This one is among the oldest surviving bombers in the world, and one of the very few remaining multi-engine aircraft from WWI.

AIRCRAFT SPECIFICATIONS

Wingspan:	17.2 m (56 ft 5 in)
Length:	7.2 m (23 ft 8 in)
Height:	2.6 m (8 ft 6 in)
Weight, empty:	733 kg (1,616 lb)
Weight, gross:	1,232 kg (2,716 lb)
Top speed:	132 km/h (82 mph)
Engines:	two Le Rhône 9C, 80 hp
Armament:	two .30 caliber Lewis machine guns
Manufacturer:	Caudron Frères, Issy-les-Moulineaux, France, 1916

TOP
The NASM's Caudron G.4 on display in the Smithsonian's Arts and Industries Building shortly after World War I.

BOTTOM LEFT
Caudron G.4 in flight at Issy-les-Moulineaux, site of the Caudron Factory.

BOTTOM RIGHT
Caudron G.4 in Dutch markings, with orange national insignia on white rudder.

RIGHT AND BELOW
The Garber team details the interior
and wing of the L-5. Beautiful wood
structures and a simple cockpit design
are only visible during a full restoration.
The L-5 was the last complete aircraft
restoration accomplished at the Paul E.
Garber Restoration Facility before the
move to the Udvar-Hazy Center.

Stinson L-5
Sentinel

Versatile, durable, and an important aircraft of World War II
the L-5 flew a wide variety of missions: photo reconnaissance, resupply, evacuation of wounded, message courier,
VIP transport, and artillery spotting. Its design was roughly
derived from the prewar Stinson Model 105 Voyager. The
Army Air Corps purchased six Voyagers from Vultee Aircraft
(which had acquired Stinson) in 1941 for testing. Refitted
with the Lycoming O-435-1 engine, the aircraft was designated the Model 75. While it had features and components
of the Voyager series, it was fundamentally a new design.

The Army ordered this model in quantity, designating
it first as the O-62 ("O" for observation), then as the L-5
("L" for liaison) when the type designation was changed
in 1942. This aircraft was the first O-62/L-5 produced.

AIRCRAFT SPECIFICATIONS

Wingspan:	10.4 m (34 ft)
Length:	7.3 m (24 ft 1 in)
Height:	2.1 m (7 ft 1 in)
Weight, empty:	703 kg (1,550 lb)
Weight, gross:	916 kg (2,020 lb)
Top speed:	185 km/h (115 mph)
Engine:	Lycoming O-435-1, horizontally opposed 6-cylinder, 185 hp
Crew:	2
Manufacturer:	Consolidated Vultee, Stinson Div., Wayne, Mich., 1942

ABOVE
The L-5 is displayed in the "Brodie" configuration. This unique launch and recovery system allowed the
aircraft to penetrate austere locations by launching from mobile small ships or even by "landing" in rough
terrain on a tightrope-like wire system.

TOP
NASM's aircraft is the first production model of the L-5—originally numbered the O-62. The "L" stood for "Liaison" while the "O" stood for "Observation."

BOTTOM
The L-5 pilot and observer had to climb down to the aircraft before takeoff and reverse the procedure after landing.

Space Shuttle (OV-101) *Enterprise*

Named like the ship of *Star Trek* lore, the first space shuttle orbiter *Enterprise* signaled a new mode of space transportation. *Enterprise* rolled out of Rockwell International's assembly facility in Palmdale, California, in 1976. In 1977, it entered service at NASA's Dryden Flight Research Center, Edwards Air Force Base, for a series of atmospheric test flights. The shuttle was flown atop its Boeing 747 carrier aircraft and also released for piloted free-flights and landings to test systems and aerodynamic performance.

 Enterprise was not equipped for spaceflight; it lacked propulsion and thermal protection systems that were not needed for the flight and ground tests. Although *Enterprise* never flew in space, its service as a test vehicle prepared the way for the other orbiters. *Enterprise* heralded the beginning of the shuttle era. In 1985, NASA transferred *Enterprise* to the Smithsonian National Air and Space Museum.

VEHICLE SPECIFICATIONS

Wingspan:	23.77 m (78 ft)
Length:	37.19 m (122 ft)
Height:	17.37 m (57 ft)
Weight:	68,000 kg (150,000 lb)
Engine:	none
Crew:	2
Manufacturer:	Rockwell International, Calif.

TOP
Enterprise rests patiently in temporary storage at Dulles International Airport surrounded by many other air and space artifacts.

BOTTOM LEFT
Rollout of *Enterprise* at Rockwell, the vehicle's manufacturer, in 1976.

BOTTOM CENTER
Actors from the television series *Star Trek* join the festivities at the rollout ceremony.

BOTTOM RIGHT
The *Enterprise* test crews and the OV-101 test shuttle. Only two crewmen were on board during each test flight.

OPPOSITE TOP LEFT
The James S. McDonnell Space Hangar (shown under construction) will house *Enterprise* and many other historic space artifacts.

OPPOSITE CENTER LEFT
Enterprise separates from the 747 that carried the shuttle to altitude for glide testing.

OPPOSITE BOTTOM LEFT
A shuttle cockpit in the original configuration, before "glass cockpit" upgrades.

OPPOSITE BOTTOM RIGHT
Successful completion of a glide test is celebrated by a unique flyby combination of T-38 chase planes and the 747 carrier aircraft.

OPPOSITE TOP RIGHT
The shuttle *Enterprise* being hoisted into position for vibration tests at NASA Marshall Space Flight Center in Alabama.

OPPOSITE CENTER RIGHT
Enterprise undergoes a "fit check" with the large liquid propellant tank and the twin solid rocket boosters on the launch pad at Kennedy Space Center in Florida.

APPROACH AND LANDING TEST
HAISE · FULLERTON
ENGLE · TRULY
USA
Enterprise

Restoration

THE PAUL E. GARBER Preservation, Restoration, and Storage Facility is where the rubber meets the road and the hard work of rebuilding and saving the nation's air and space artifact collections takes place. To all of us at NASM, it is simply called "Garber."

The facility is named in honor of Paul Edward Garber, (1899–1992) who was instrumental in collecting more than half of the Smithsonian-owned aircraft on display at the facility named in his honor, at the National Air and Space Museum (NASM) on the mall and, on loan, at other museums around the world. He fell under the spell of both aviation and the Smithsonian while growing up in Washington, D.C. As a 10-year-old, he took a streetcar across the Potomac to watch Orville Wright fly the world's first military airplane at Fort Myer, Virginia.

The Garber Facility is a no-frills assembly of about 30 metal buildings belonging to the National Air and Space Museum and other Smithsonian organizations. About 19 buildings are crammed full of airplanes, spacecraft, and a wide variety of associated parts. One building is devoted to a large restoration shop and 3 buildings are for exhibition production. Each artifact at the Garber Facility has a story behind it. Some are notable for a certain historical role they played or for a particular accomplishment; some represent a technological milestone or stage of aeronautical development; some are the sole surviving example of their type. Often an artifact is worth collecting for a combination of reasons. Soon, the majority of these artifacts will reside in the new Udvar-Hazy Center for all to enjoy for the first time since they were collected decades ago.

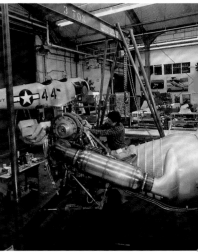

Gift Wrapped for America

BY THE TIME THE STEVEN F. UDVAR-HAZY CENTER opens on December 15, 2003, more aircraft will have been moved, hung, and polished than at any other time since the National Air and Space Museum opened on the National Mall in 1976. Nearly 80 aviation and space artifacts await visitors on that day. But the best is yet to come. By the time the Center is filled, more than 300 aircraft and spacecraft, thousands of artifacts and dozens of small exhibits will enrich and inspire visitors from around the world.

While the aircraft and spacecraft await the opening events, they have been wrapped in protective plastic so that cleaning and dusting is kept to a minimum as the opening nears. At the time this book was assembled, the Udvar-Hazy Center resembled more an enormous child's bedroom—aircraft tacked carefully to the ceiling and models placed in selected spaces on dressers and desks. But this place contains real planes and spaceships and they have all been prepared for America and the world to enjoy.

RIGHT
The Vought F4U-1D Corsair seems ready to land on a carrier deck.

FAR RIGHT
The Turner RT-14 shown with Roscoe Turner's lion, Gilmore.

BELOW
The Curtiss P-40E Warhawk (Kittyhawk IA) is hoisted into position.

OPPOSITE TOP
The aircraft in the aeronautics hangar are gift wrapped in plastic awaiting the Udvar-Hazy Center opening in December 2003.

OPPOSITE BOTTOM
The Chipmunk as it appeared in flight.

ABOVE RIGHT
The Mikoyan-Gurevich MiG-15 (Ji-2) FAGOT B shines while awaiting visitors.

RIGHT
The Okha-22 Cherry Blossom, built for war, is the last one that remains in the world.

The North American F-86A Sabre, America's most formidable fighter over the skies of Korea, is restored and will inspire all who view it at the Udvar-Hazy Center.

Library of Congress Control Number: 2003111746

ISBN: 0-9745113-0-7

Front cover: The Museum's Lockheed SR-71A Blackbird
Back cover: Space shuttle (OV-101) *Enterprise*

Photo credits:
Images from Smithsonian National Air and Space Museum (NASM) with the exception of the following: Alan D. Toelle via NASM, page 45; Bell Helicopter Textron via NASM, page 20; The Boeing Company via NASM, page 34; Bombardier, Inc. via NASM, page 46 (lower left); Jim Qualls, pages 26–27 (graphic image, top center); National Aeronautics and Space Administration (NASA), pages 28 (center right and bottom), 29 (top left and bottom left), 52 (all), 66 (bottom), 67 (all except top left); Shell Companies Foundation, Inc. via NASM, page 61 (lower right)

Edited by the staff of the National Air and Space Museum
Proofread by Laura Iwasaki and Marie Weiler
Designed by Jeff Wincapaw
Color separations by iocolor, Seattle
Produced by Marquand Books, Inc., Seattle
    www.marquand.com
Printed and bound by C&C Offset Printing Co., Ltd., China